Learn to Sing Do-Re-Mi Level One Contents

Learn to Sing Do-Re-Mi Level One Contents

Adapted for Disabilities Introduction

Created by: Sarah Samuelson

Learn to Sing Do-Re-Mi is a curriculum for learning how to read music by singing. I have created this version out of love for my students with disabilities in order to help other teachers and parents bring the joy of music to their students. Be sure to adapt as needed.

1) **Practice vowel recognition by singing solfège** – The solfège method assigns each note in the music scale with a syllable: do-re-mi-fa-so-la-ti-do as heard in the song "doe a deer...ray a drop of golden sun...me a name I call myself." This curriculum introduces the syllables slowly, starting only with do-re-mi for the first nine songs, giving consistent repetition for students needing practice with verbal skills. I have witnessed incredible verbal growth by students.

2) **Practice doing the hand signs:** For some students it can be best for you to do the singing and the student does the hand signs with you. Hand signs are in every song.

3) **Do the motions in the songs with physical movements**: The Do-Re-Mi Body Tap song has students tap knees, belly and chest for the pitches. "You are Important" is song is a falling down song students love. It is similar to a ring-around-the-rosie song with better lyrics. Leap for Joy is a jumping song. And remember, these may be the only songs you do for awhile. I use large saucer-sized cut front felt notes in the colors (red for do) that the students enjoy putting on their knees. Repetition is key.

4) **Practice eye tracking** – The colors and large print in this edition help students to track the notes and words. I recommend using a print edition so students can physically track the notes. I point for them until they are able to themselves. Even if the student has difficulty tracking with eyes, there is so much to learn by ear.

5) **Reinforce color recognition with Boomwhackers** – Boomwhackers are colored tubes of different lengths with a different color for every pitch. Each song in Level One is introduced with the notes being the colors of the tubes. Boomwhackers are easy to tap or play with a mallet. We practice "ready position" and "resting position." Ready, is holding it up and waiting for every one to be ready. Resting is gently resting the tube on the floor.

6) **Learn about empathy** – These songs are great for teaching what it means to have empathy, understand emotions, and appreciate diversity. Remember some students do best with singing only the do-re-mi, but they enjoy hearing the other words.

7) **Combine singing with other therapies and exercises** - One method for building additional skills in eye tracking and hand-eye coordination that combines well with music is a program called Bal-a-Vis-X. This program consists of 200+ exercises, each rooted deeply in rhythm. They range in difficulty from one hand passing/receiving a single sandbag to both hands bouncing/catching four racquetballs in a specified sequence. Others combine bags or balls with feet exercises. Each of the exercises in Bal-a-Vis-X address visual tracking deficiencies and auditory imprecision, impulsivity, balance and anxiety issues. See www.bal-a-vis-x.com.

Lesson 1: Rhythm

walk   walk   walk   walk

jog - ging,   jog - ging,   jog - ging   jog - ging,

walk   walk   walk   walk

TEACHER NOTES

Speak the words in a steady beat to get to know the timing of the notes. Speak the words as you walk and jog and keep a steady beat. Notice the bar line and the double bar line at the ends of the staffs.

2

Rhythm in Speech

red red red red

or- ange, or- ange, o - range o - range

Rhythm in Silence

red (silence) red (silence)

o - range (silence) o - range (silence)

Notice the beam connecting the notes and the
repeat sign at the end of the staff.

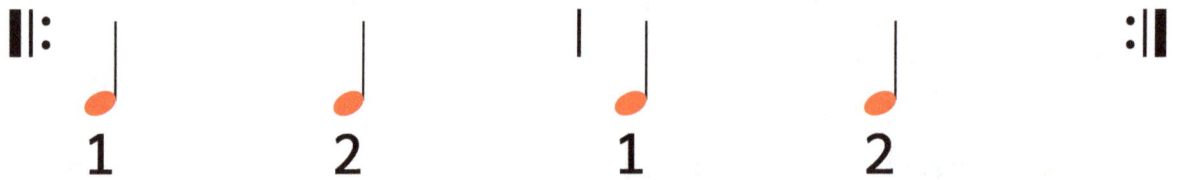

Eighth Notes

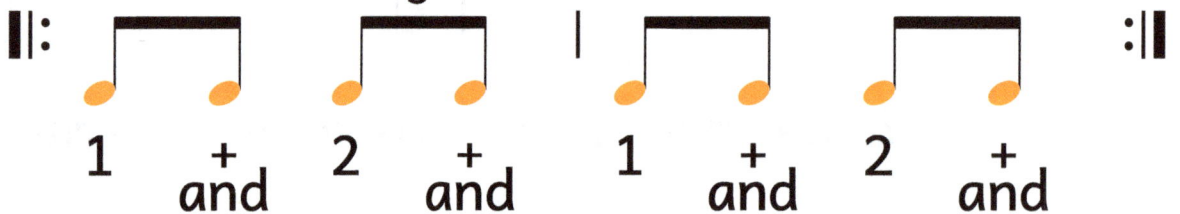

When counting quarter and eighth notes it is best to "subdivide" which means to add the "and" when counting the quarter notes so that your eighth notes can be more even.

Quarter Notes & Rests

𝄆 ♩ 𝄽 | ♩ 𝄽 𝄇

1　+　2　+　　1　+　2　+
　　　(silence)　　　　(silence)

Eighth Notes & Rests

𝄆 ♫ 𝄾 | ♫ 𝄾 𝄇

1　+　2　+　1　+　2　+

Quarter Notes & Eighth Notes & Rests

𝄆 ♩ 𝄾 | ♫ 𝄾 𝄇

1　+　2　+　1　+　2　+

Solfège C Major Scale with Boomwhacker Colors To

C

do re mi fa so la ti do

Solfège C Major Scale for Piano

Middle C

do re mi fa so la ti do

Chords for Piano

C   G7   F

Lesson 2: do
We are Part of this Beautiful World
Music: Sarah Samuelson

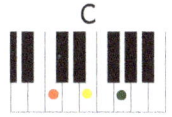

We are Part of this Beautiful World

Music: Sarah Samuelson

C

We are part of this

beau – ti – ful world where

ev – 'ry – one has worth.

When a word has three syllables
so there will be three notes.

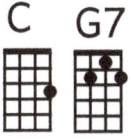

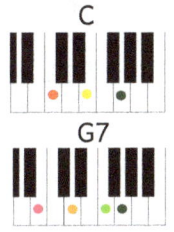

Lesson 3: do & re
I Have Worth
Music: Sarah Samuelson

C	G⁷		C		C	G⁷	C	
do	re		do	do	do	re	do	

C	G⁷		C		C		C	
do	re		do	do		do	do	do

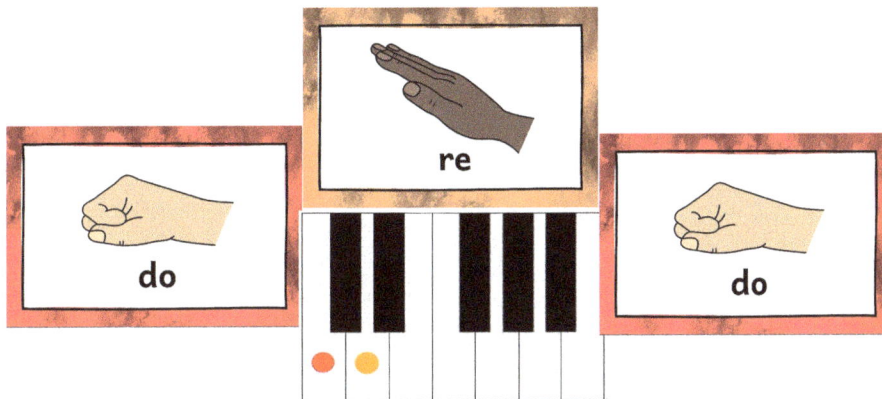

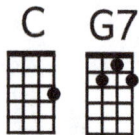

I Have Worth

Text & Music: Sarah Samuelson

C G7 C C G7 C

I be - lieve that I have worth.

C G7 C C

I be - lieve that you have worth.

Lesson 4: do & re
I Can Show Empathy

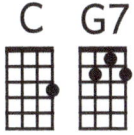
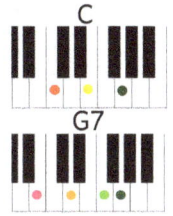

C | G7 | C | G7 | C

do do re | do do do | do re | do do

C | G7 | C | G7 | C

do do re | do do do | do re | do do

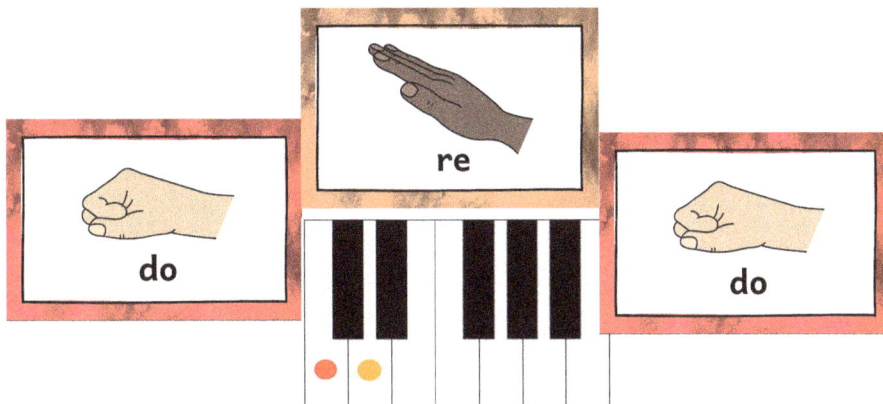

do — re — do

I Can Show Empathy

Text & Music: Sarah Samuelson

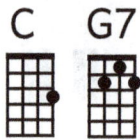

C   G⁷   C

I can show em – pa – thy:

G⁷   C

I see your view.

C   G⁷   C

I can show em – pa – thy:

C   G⁷   C

I feel with you.

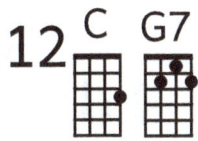

Lesson 5: do-re-mi
Do-Re-Mi Body Tap
Music: Sarah Samuelson

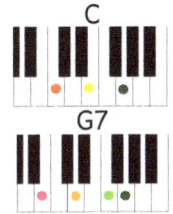

C — Tap your knees and say: do do do

G⁷ — Tap your tum-my: re re re re

C — Tap your chest: mi mi mi

C — mi mi re re **G⁷** do **C** do do do do

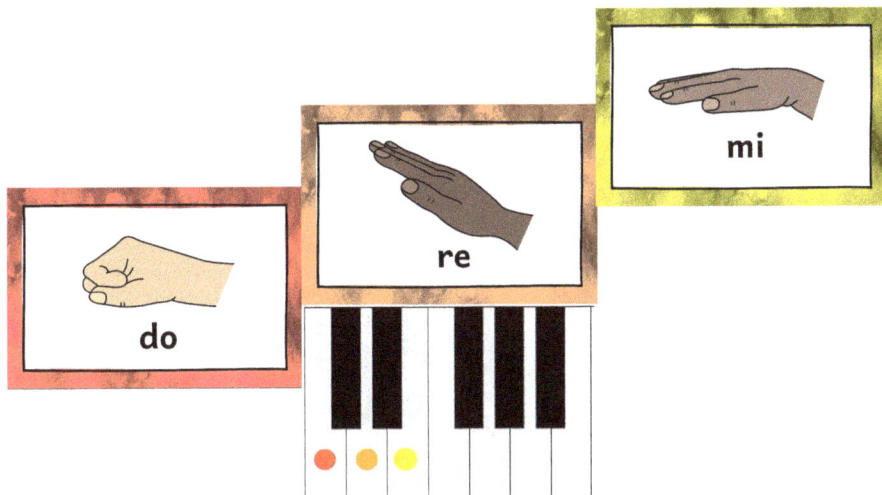

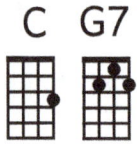

Do-Re-Mi Body Tap
Music: Sarah Samuelson

14

Words Can Be Healing to Say

Text & Music: Sarah Samuelson

C

My words can give a smile to you.

G7

Your words help me see a-no-ther view.

C

Words can help a hurt go a-way.

C **G7** **C**

Words can be heal-ing to say.

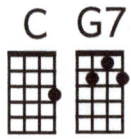

Lesson 6: do-re-mi

Welcome Here

Music: English Round (Hot Cross Buns)

15

C	G⁷	C			C	G⁷	C	
mi	re	do	do	do	mi	re	do	

C		G⁷			C	G⁷	C	
do	do	re	re	re	re	mi	re	do

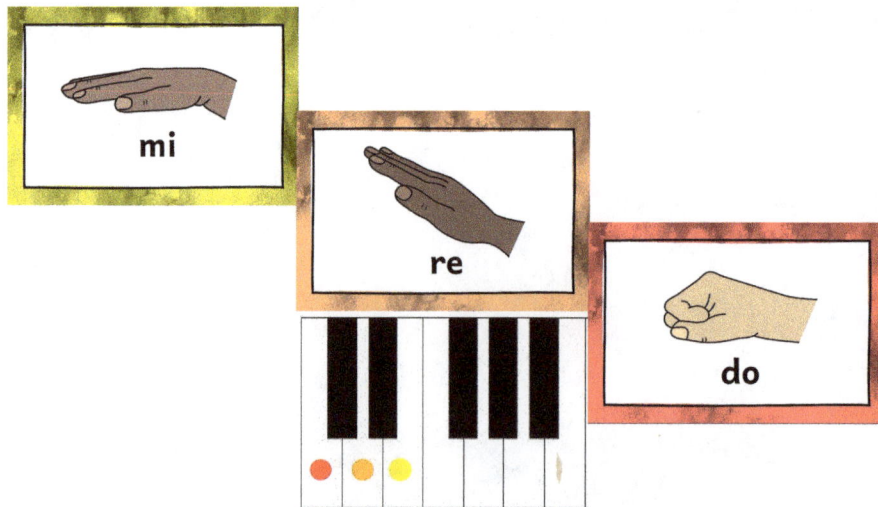

Welcome Here

Music: English Round (Hot Cross Buns)

16

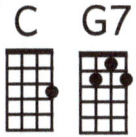

We want all to feel

wel - come here.

We va - lue the cul - ture of each

per - son here.

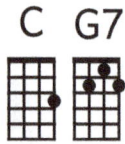

Lesson 7: do-mi

I Can Be a Friend

Music: France (Au Clair de la Lune)

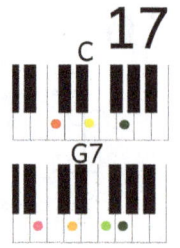

C G7

C				G⁷		C	G⁷		C	
do	do	do	re	mi	re	do	mi	re	do	do

C				G⁷		C	G⁷		C	
do	do	do	re	mi	re	do	mi	re	re	do	do

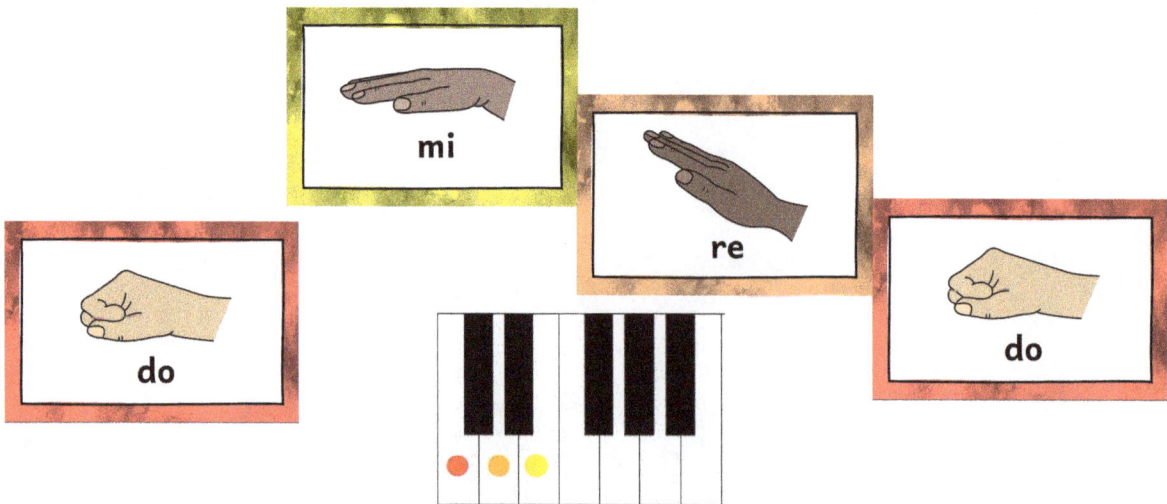

mi

re

do

do

18 C G7

I Can Be a Friend
Music: France (Au Clair de la Lune)

C   G7

I   can   be   a   friend   and

C   G7   C

take   some   time   to   lis – ten.

G7

This   is   one   way   I   can

C   G7   C

show   my   friend   com – pas – sion.

Lesson 8: do-mi
Leap for Joy
Music: Folk Song: Hop Old Squirrel

C

mi mi mi   mi mi mi mi   re do

G⁷ C

C

mi mi mi   mi mi mi mi   re re

G⁷

C

mi mi mi   mi mi mi mi   re re do

G⁷ C

C

mi mi mi   re re re re   do do do

G⁷   C

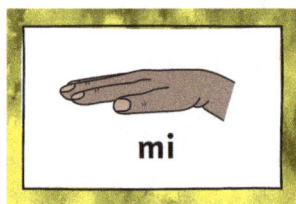
mi

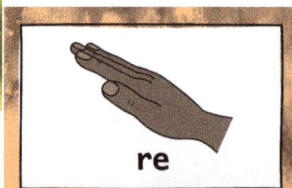
re

do

Copyright © 2024 Sarah Samuelson Studio

Leap for Joy

Music: Folk Song (Hop Old Squirrel)

20 — C G7

Line 1: (C ... G7 C)
Leap for joy! We're u-nique and spe- cial!

Line 2: (C ... G7)
Leap for joy! grate-ful to be lear- ning!

Line 3: (C ... G7 C)
Leap for joy! We each have some thing to give!

Line 4: (C ... G7 C)
Leap for joy! We can be en-cou-ra- ging!

Lesson 9: do-mi
I Can Be More Understanding
Music: Spiritual (Babylon's Falling)

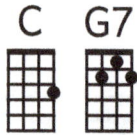

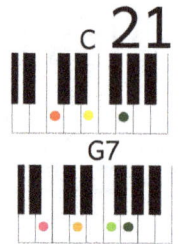

do do mi do re do do mi do

do do mi do re re do do

I Can Be More Understanding

Music: African American Spiritual (Babylon's Falling)

I can learn to solve ma-ny pro-blems.

I can be more un-der-stan-ding.

Put Yourself in Their Shoes

Text: Danielle Coke Balfour; Music: Spiritual (Oh, I'm Goin' to Sing)

C   G7

so   mi mi mi mi   re re re re   do do do

re re re re   mi mi so   mi re   do

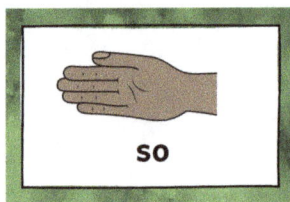

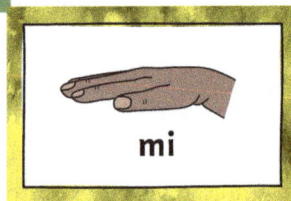

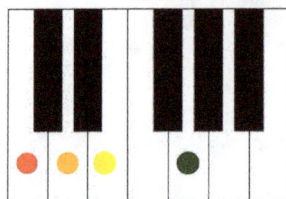

24

Put Yourself in Their Shoes
Text: Danielle Coke Balfour; Music: Spiritual (Oh, I'm Goin' to Sing)

It should-nt have to hap-pen to you

for it to mat – ter to you

Put your-self in their shoes.

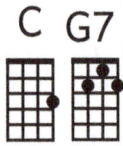
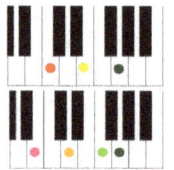

We Want All to Feel Connected
Music: USA (Mary Had a Little Lamb)

C | **G⁷**
mi re do re mi mi mi re re re re

C | **C**
mi so so so mi re do re mi mi

G⁷ | **C**
mi mi re re mi re do do do

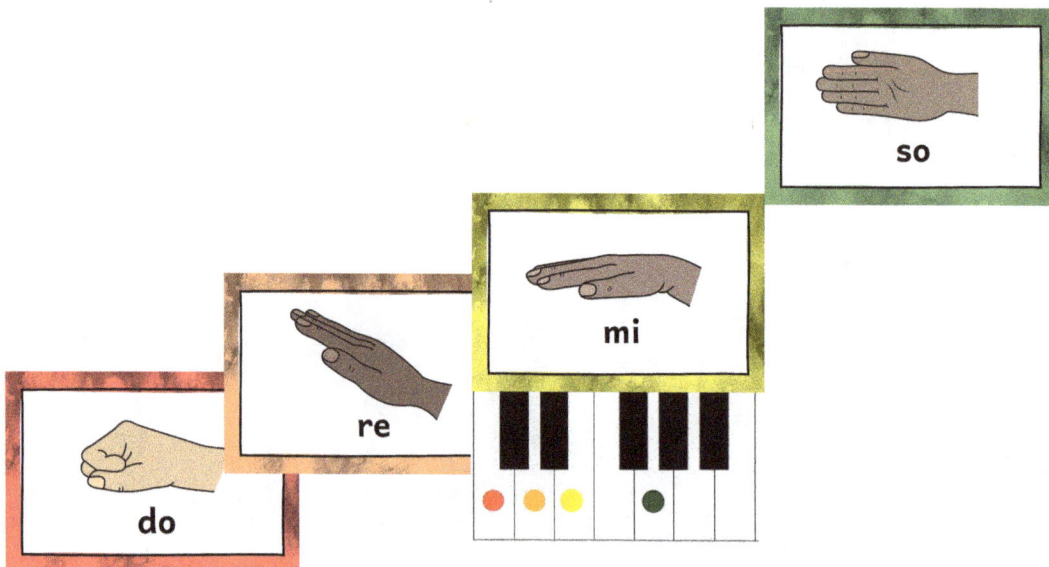

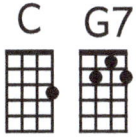

We Want All to Feel Connected
Music: USA (Mary Had a Little Lamb)

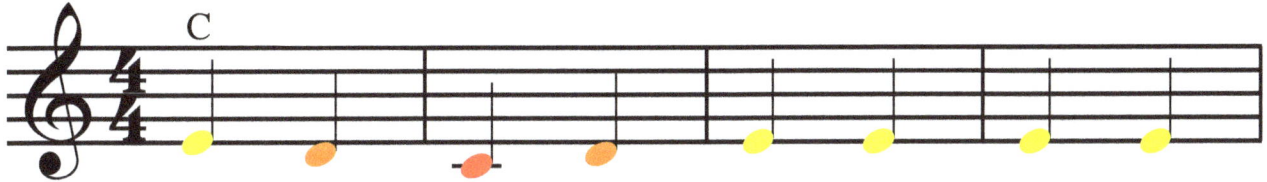

We want all to feel con - nec - ted,

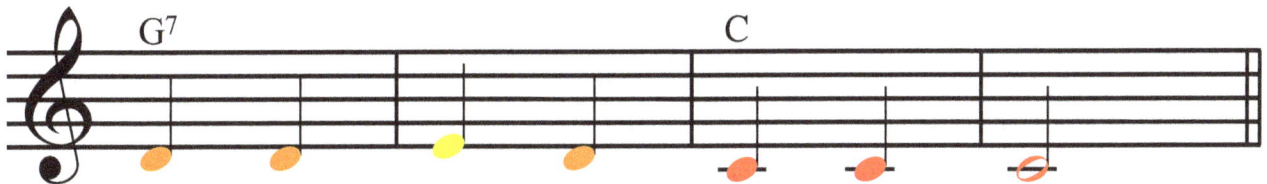

when in - clu - ded, and re - spec - ted.

We want all to feel con - nec - ted

in our own com - mu - ni - ty.

Lesson 12: re-so
We Each Have a Family
Music: USA (Johnny Works with One Hammer)

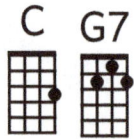

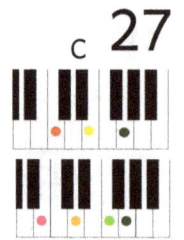

do do do mi so so mi mi mi

re re so so mi mi do

do do do do mi so so mi

re re so so mi do

We Each Have a Family

Music: USA (Johnny Works with One Hammer)

We each have a fa - mi - ly, our tra-
di - tions, cul - ture, lan - gua - ges.
Talk-ing a - bout our fa - mi - lies
helps us feel con - nec - ted.

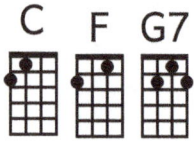

Lesson 13: so-mi
Little Changes Make a Difference
Music: Robert Lowry

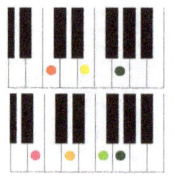

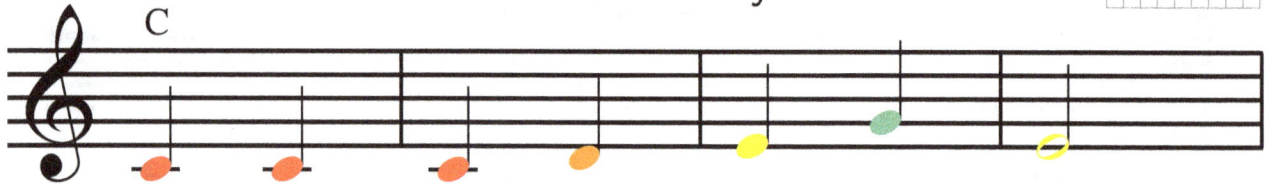

do do do re mi so mi

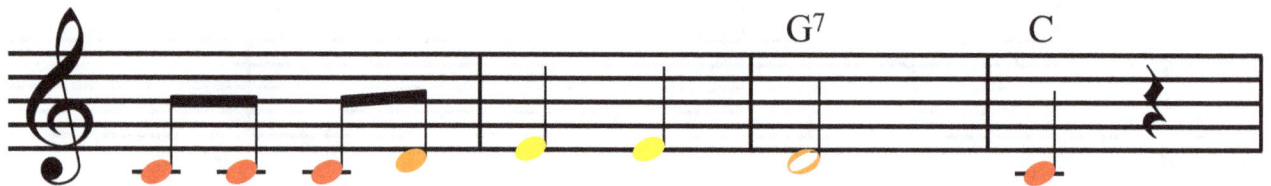

do do do re mi mi re do

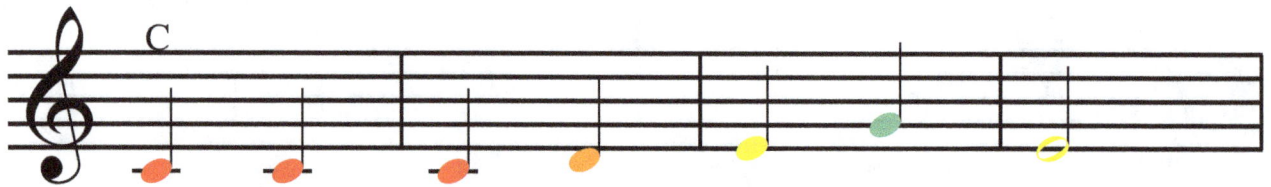

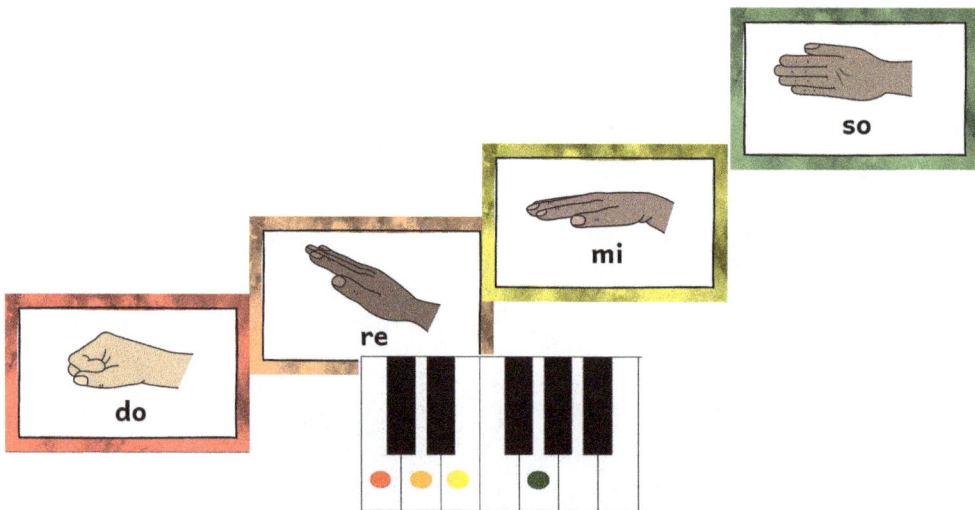

do do do re mi so mi

do do do re mi mi re do

C G7
so mi re mi so mi re re do
C C G7
re re mi so so mi re mi so
G7 C
mi do do do re mi mi re do

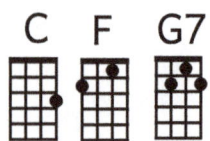

Little Changes Make a Difference

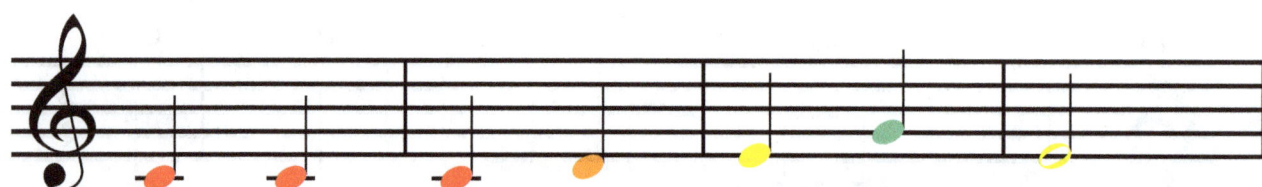

Music: Robert Lowry

Bright i - deas can form a plan

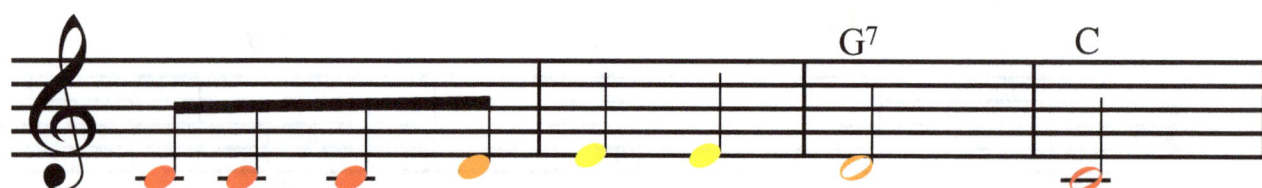

Lit tle chan-ges make a dif - ference.

Read-ing books to un - der - stand

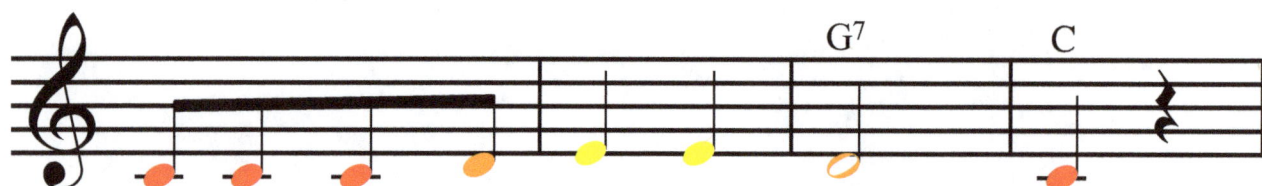

Lit-tle chan-ges make a dif - ference.

When we seek to learn what's true,

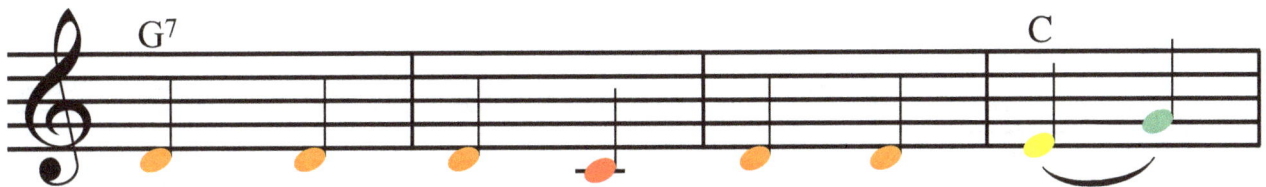

start friend ships with some-one new,

fol - low - ing the Gol - den Rule.

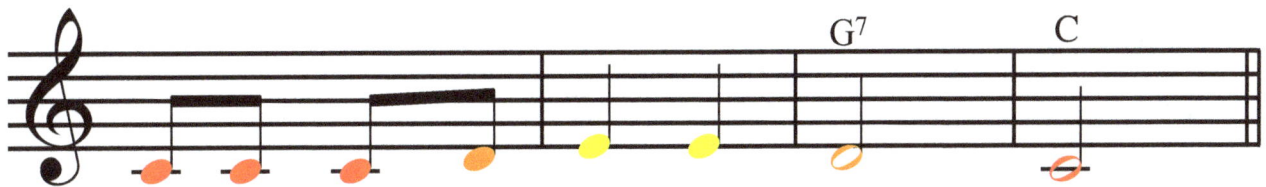

Lit-tle chan-ges make a dif - ference.

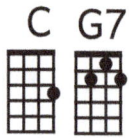

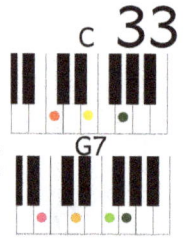

Lesson 14: fa
We're All Equal, Our Voice is Important

Music: Bohemian Folk Song

so fa mi mi re mi fa re do do

mi fa so mi re mi fa re mi fa so mi

re mi fa re so fa mi mi

re mi fa re do do

so · fa · mi · re · do

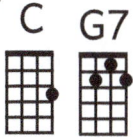

34 We're All Equal. Our Voice is Important

Music: Bohemian Folk Song (Honeybee)

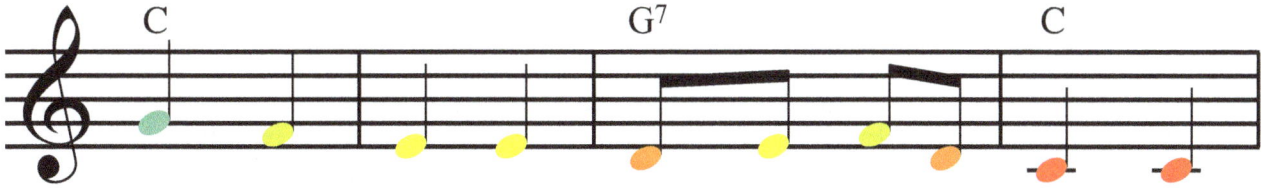

We're all e-qual. Our voice is im-por-tant.

We need to speak up and share with

ho-ne-sty and care. We're all

e-qual. Our voice is im-por-tant.

Lesson 15: fa

Stay Hopeful

Music: Sarah Samuelson

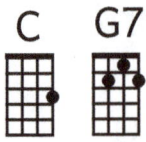

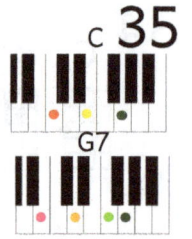

so   so   so fa mi re   so   so so   so fa mi re

so so   so fa mi re   so fa mi re   do

36 C G7

Stay Hopeful

Music: Sarah Samuelson

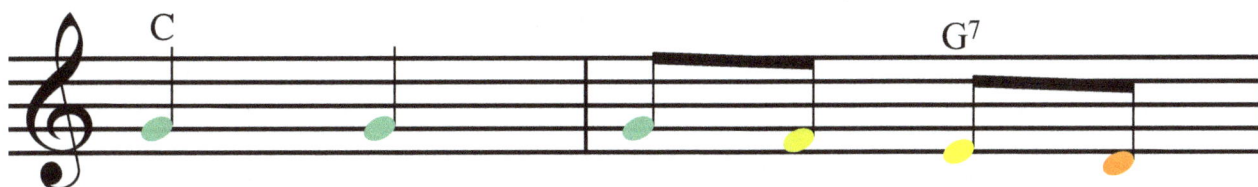

I can stay hope - ful, I'll keep on go - ing, I'm not done.

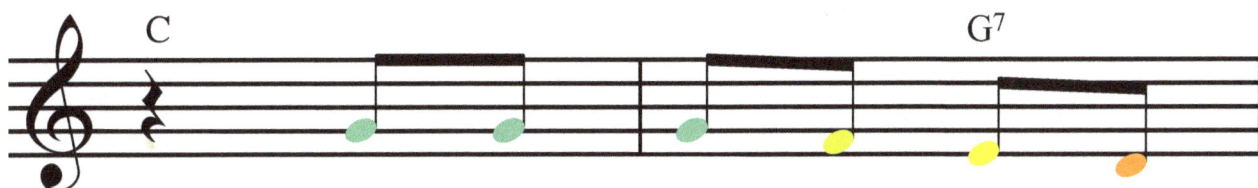

When we work to - ge - ther we can o - ver - come.

Care for my Neighbor

Music: Germany (Mäh, Lämmchen, Mäh)

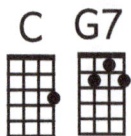

C G7

C   G7   C   G7   C

mi mi re do so so mi mi re do do so

C   G7   C   G7   C   G7

do re re mi re so do do re

C   G7   C   G7   C

mi mi re so mi do re re do

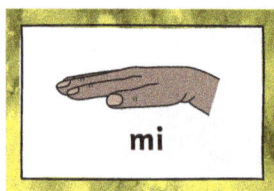

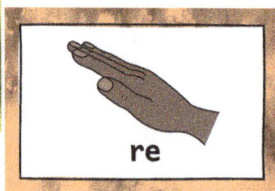

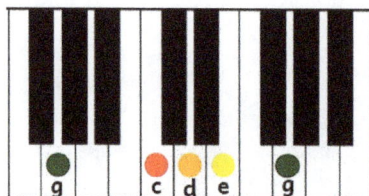

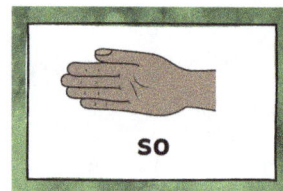

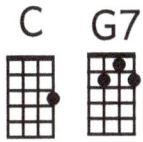

Care For My Neighbor

Music: Germany (Mäh, Lämmchen, Mäh)

I want to learn how to care for my neigh-bor, be-come more a-ware of the chal-len-ges they may face so I can be their friend.

We Want Justice in Our World

Music: Spiritual (Oh! Oh! Freedom)

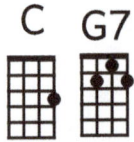

so la do do do re re mi mi

re do mi so

la do do mi re

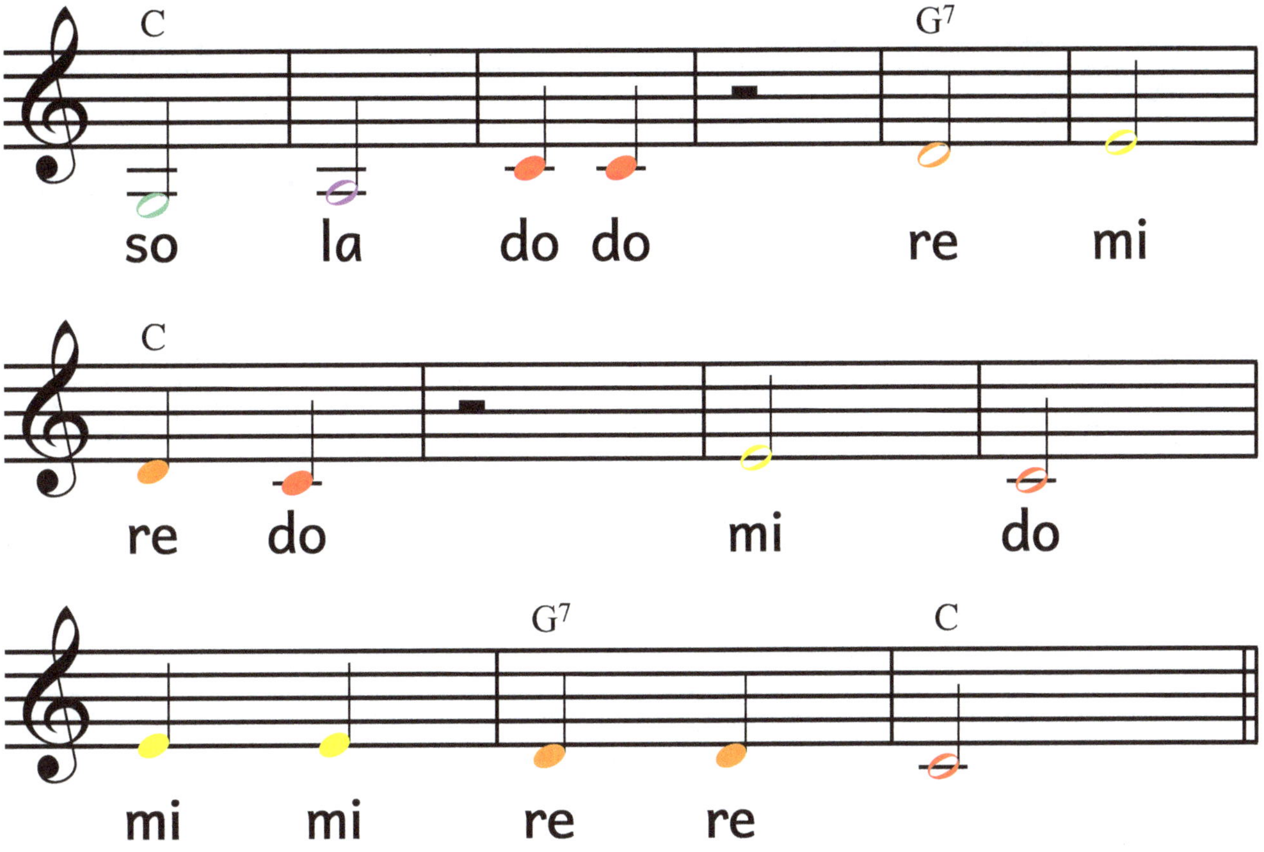
C
G7
so la do do re mi
C
re do mi do
G7
C
mi mi re re

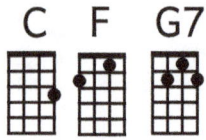

We Want Justice in Our World

Music: Spiritual (Oh! Oh! Freedom)

We want fair-ness, we look out

for each o-ther. We want ju-stice

in our world. So, we play fair,

and we show care.

We want ju-stice in our world.

Lesson 18: do,re,mi,so,la

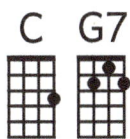

You are Important

Music: England (Here Comes a Bluebird)

C G7

so so so la so mi mi so so la so mi mi

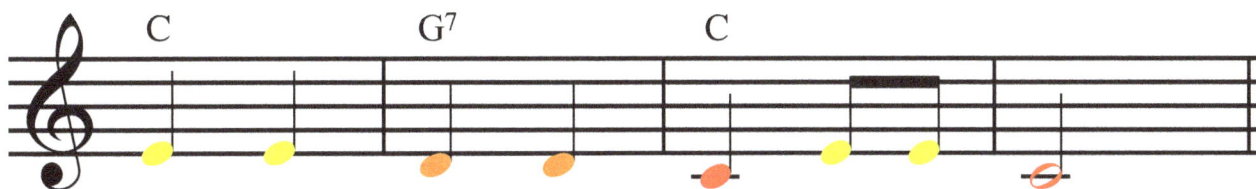

mi mi re re do mi mi do

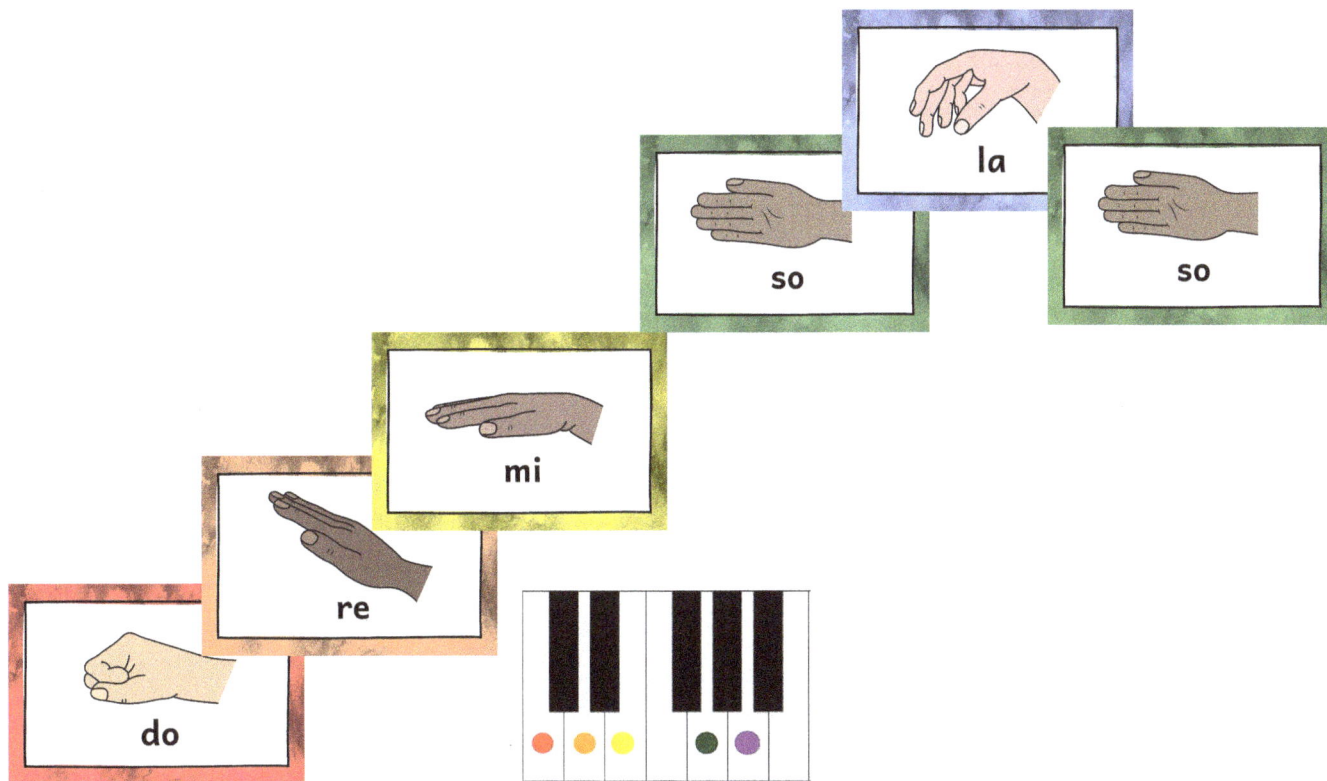

You are Important

Music: England (Here Comes a Bluebird)

C   G7

You   are im - por - tant, we   care what you're feel   -   ing.   Some   -   times you   might   fall   to   the   ground.

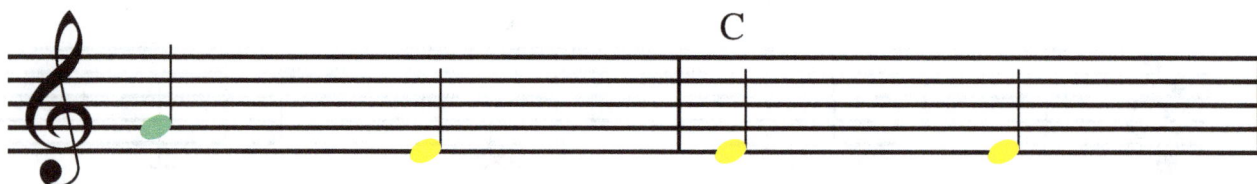

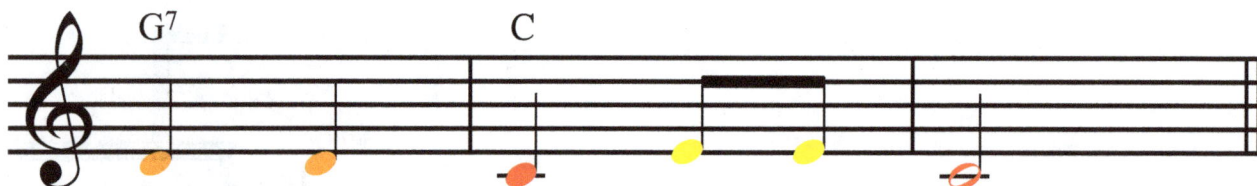

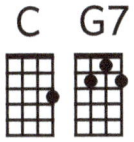

You are Important, verse 2

Music: England (Here Comes a Bluebird)

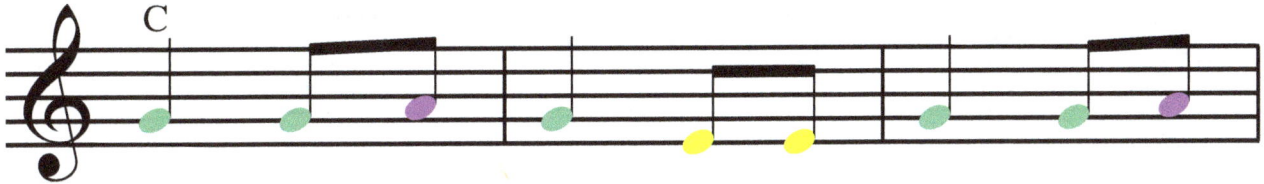

When you show care a-bout some-bo-dy's

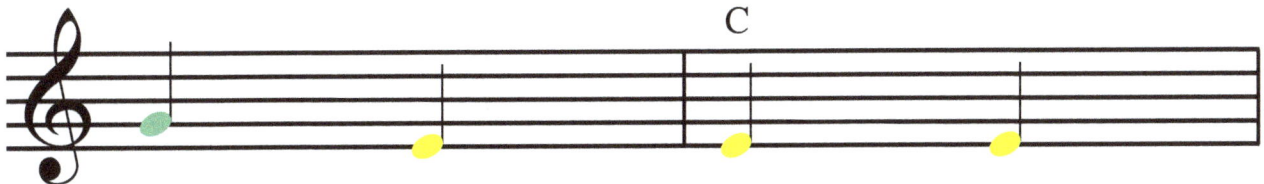

feel - ings, you can

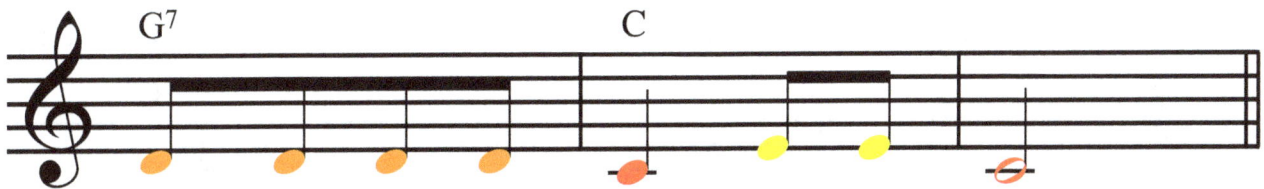

help them if they fall to the ground.

Lesson 19: fa

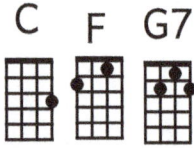

Express Our Emotions

Music: Argentina (Los elefantes)

C F G7

C

so   so   fa   mi   mi mi   so   so   fa   mi   mi

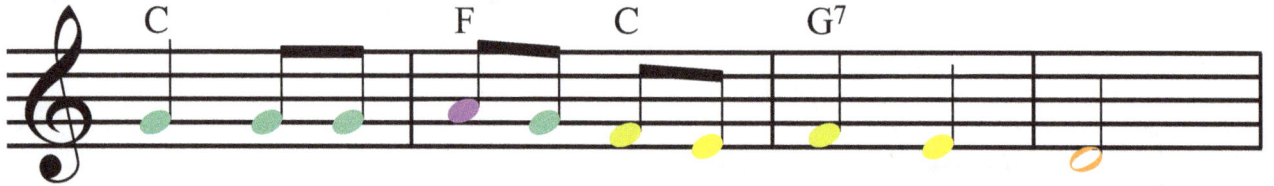

C   F   C   G⁷

so   so   so   la   so   fa   mi   fa   mi   re

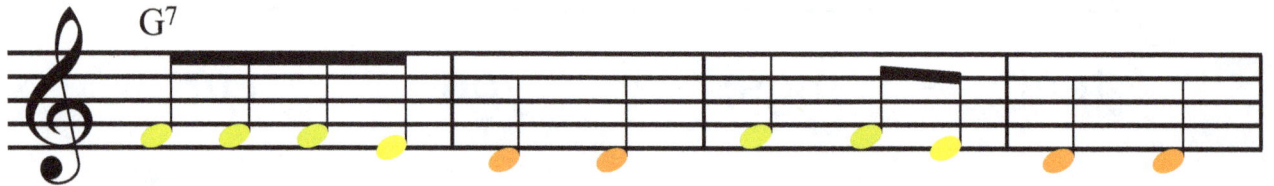

G⁷

fa   fa   fa   mi   re   re   fa   fa   mi   re   re

G⁷   C   G⁷   C

so   so   so   so   fa   mi   re   mi   re   do

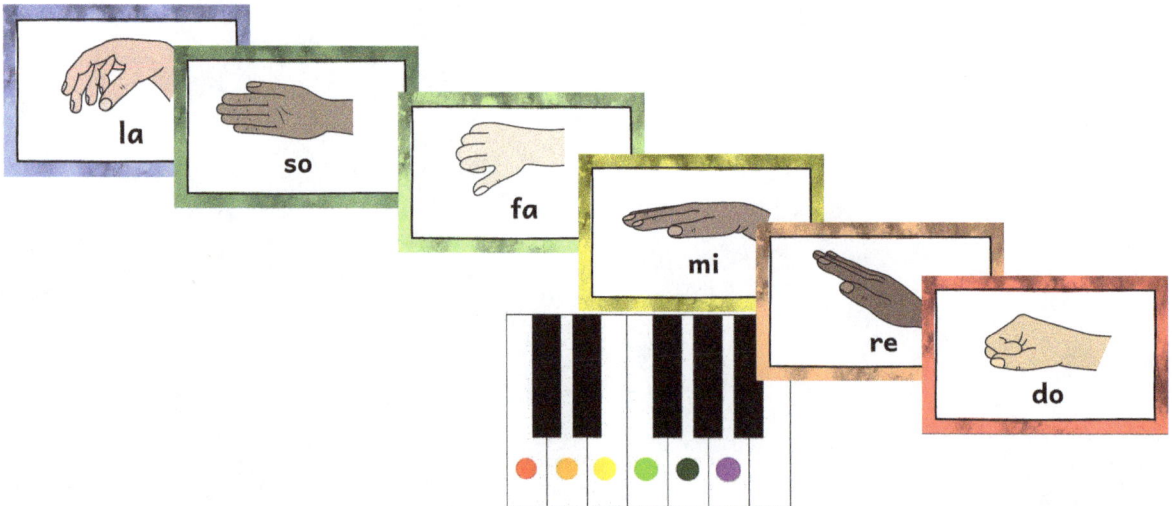

la   so   fa   mi   re   do

Express Our Emotions

Music: Argentinia (Los elefantes)

46

We can_ learn to ex press our e - mo-tions,

so we can build heal-thy friend- ships.

When we are a-ware of our e - mo-tions

we can em-pa thize and li - sten.

Lesson 20: LEAP do-so

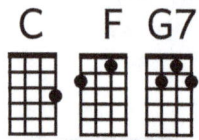

We are Like Stars in the Night

Music: Twinkle Twinkle Little Star

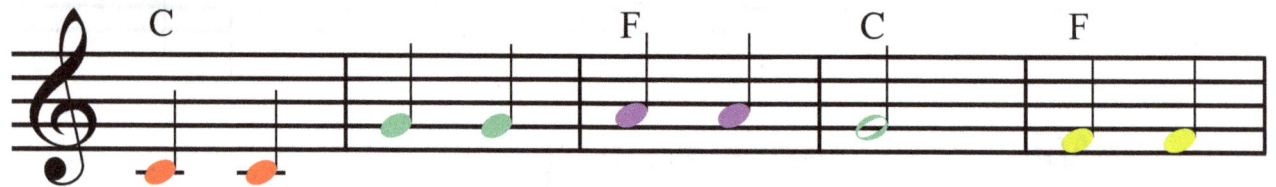

C F G7

C | **F** | **C** | **F**

do do so so la la so fa fa

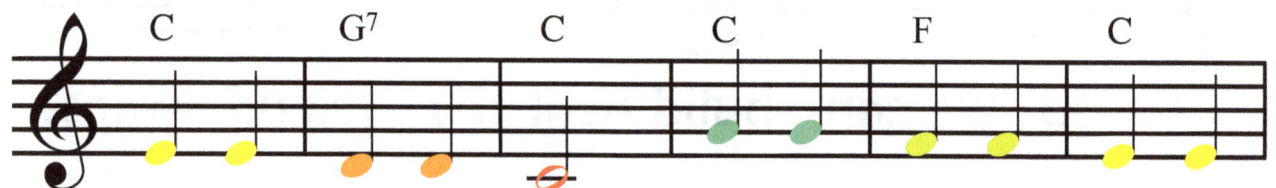

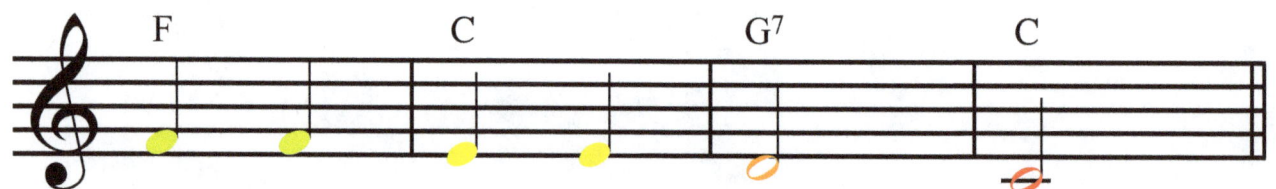

C | **G⁷** | **C** | **C** | **F** | **C**

mi mi re re do so so fa fa mi mi

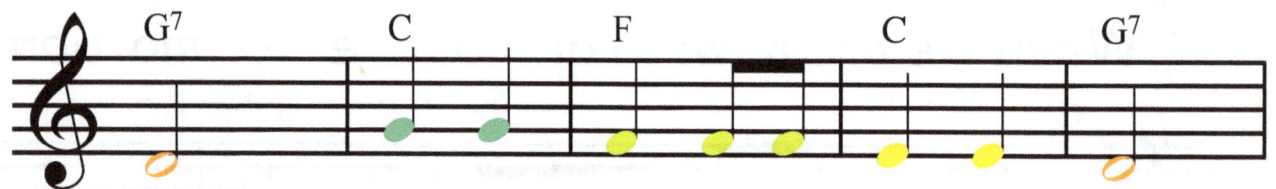

G⁷ | **C** | **F** | **C** | **G⁷**

re re so so fa fa fa mi mi re

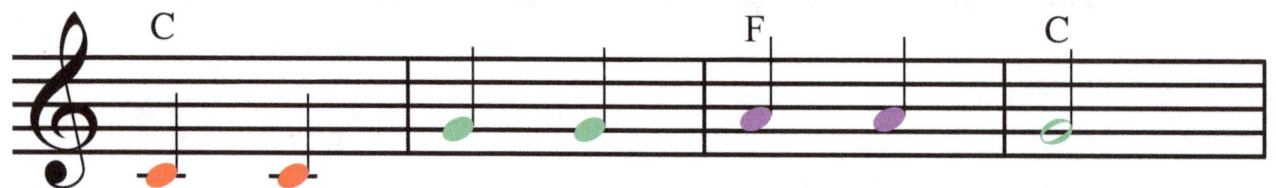

C | **F** | **C**

do do so so la la so

F | **C** | **G⁷** | **C**

fa fa mi mi re do

48 C F G7

We are Like Stars in the Night

Music: Twinkle Twinkle Little Star

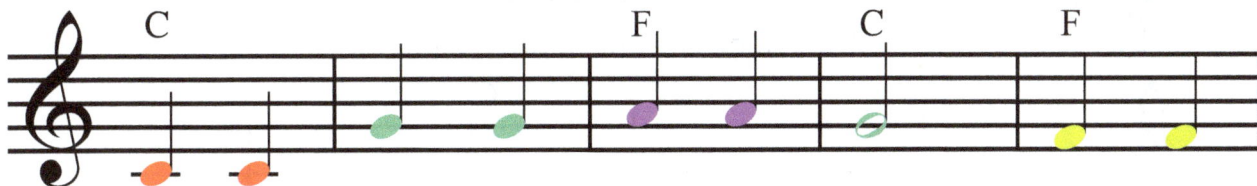

C   F   C   F

We are like stars in the night,   shi-ning

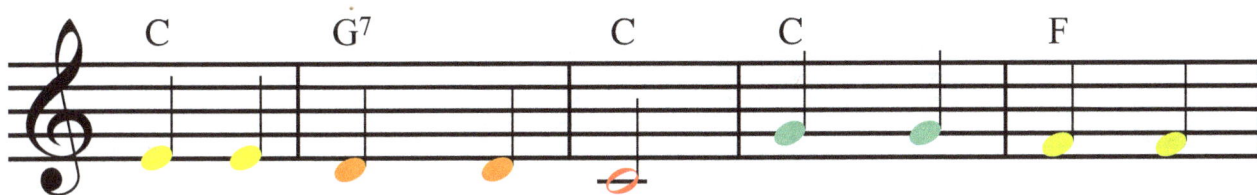

C   G7   C   C   F

on the path that's right. Peace and jus-tice,

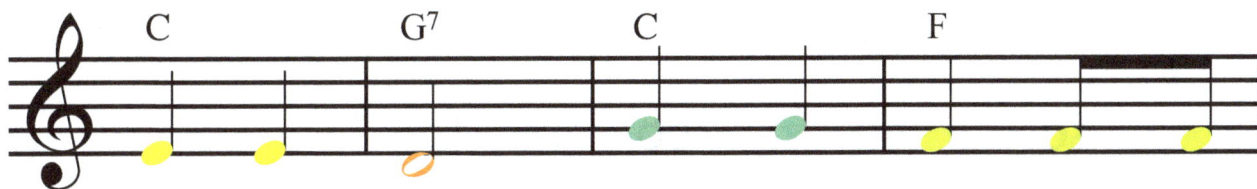

C   G7   C   F

u – ni – ty   starts with kind-ness from

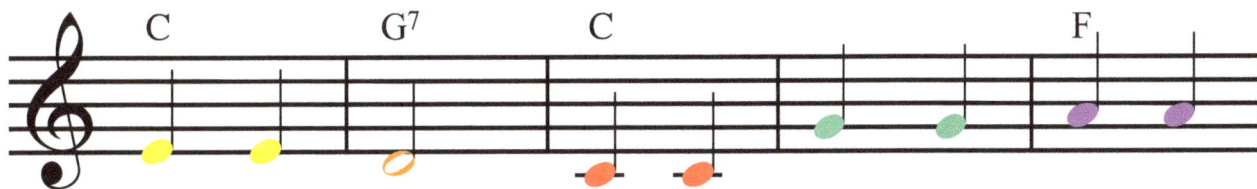

C   G7   C   F

you and me. We are like stars in the

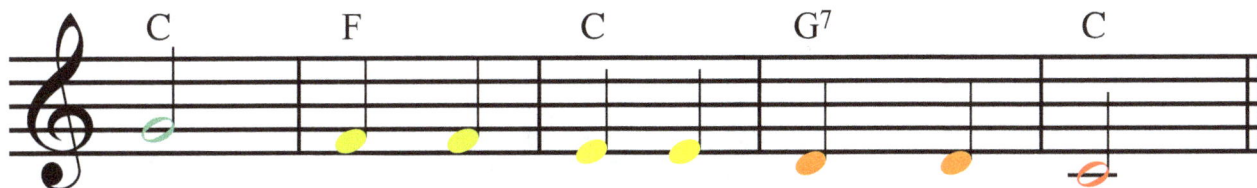

C   F   C   G7   C

night   shin-ing   on the path that's right.

Lesson 21: so-la

We All Have a Super Power

Music: Mexico (Chocolate molinillo)

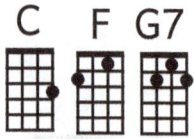

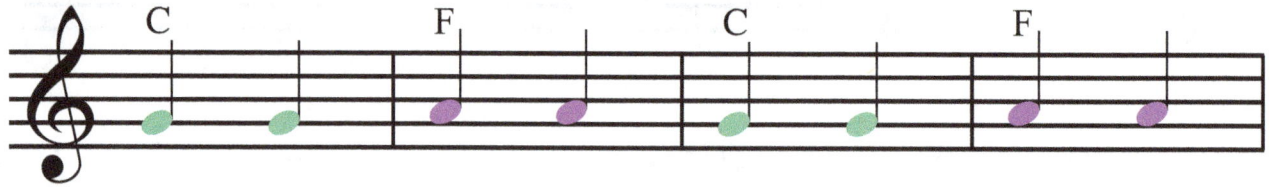

C   F   G7

C   F   C   F

so   so   la   la   so   so   la   la

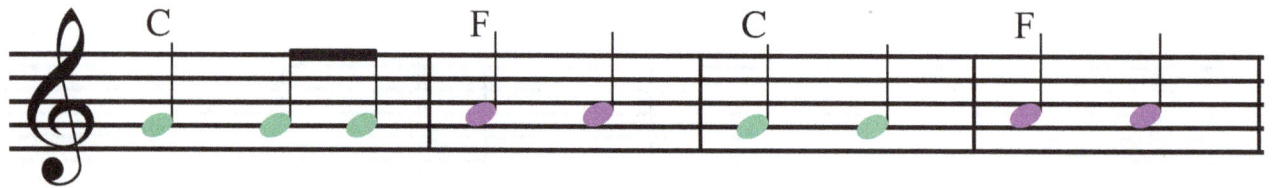

C   F   C   F

so   so   so   la   la   so   so   la   la

C

so   so   mi   fa   so   mi   fa   so   so   mi   fa

C   G⁷   C

so   fa   mi   re   do   do

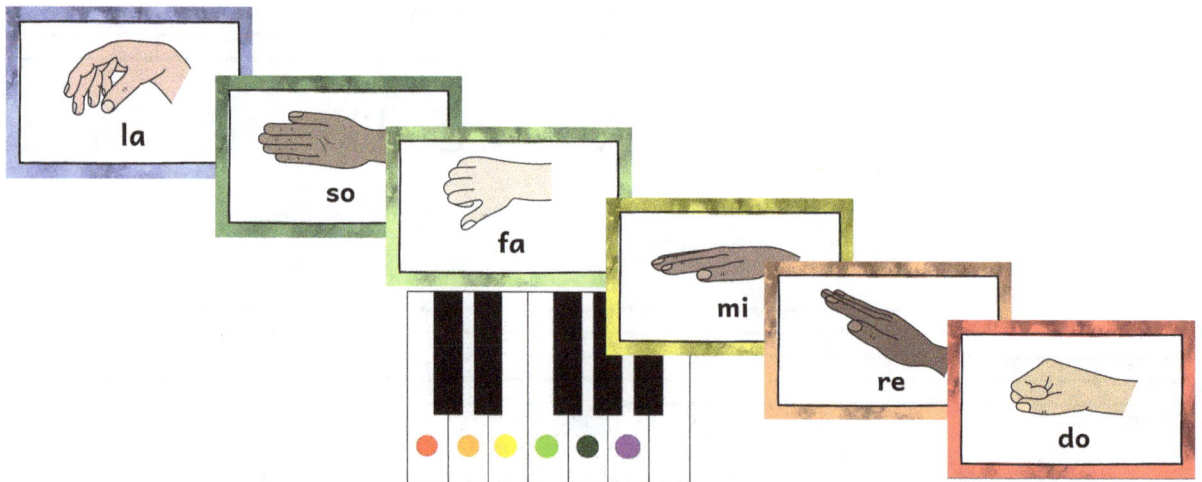

la   so   fa   mi   re   do

50 C F G7

We All Have a Super Power
Music: Mexico (Chocolate molinillo)

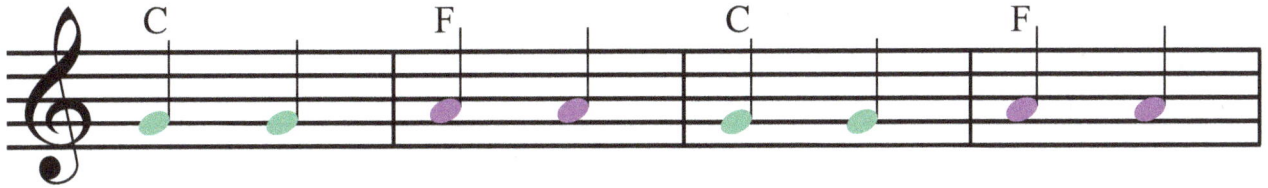

We all have a su - per po - wer!

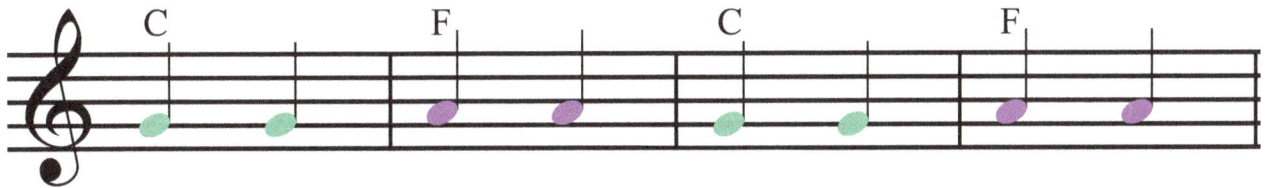

We all have a su - per po - wer!

We learn from his - tory and grow ma-king

chan - ges to help o - thers.

Lesson 22: do-re-mi-fa

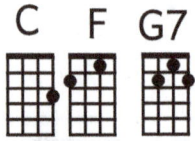

I am Learning to Regulate

Music: Japan (Kaeru nota ga)

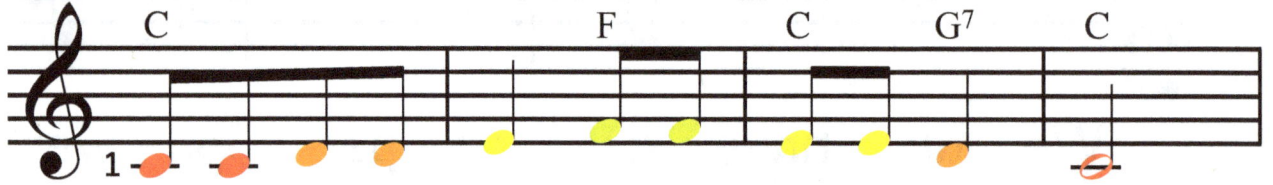

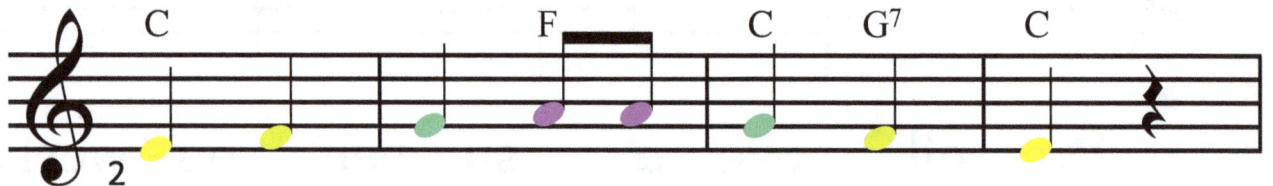

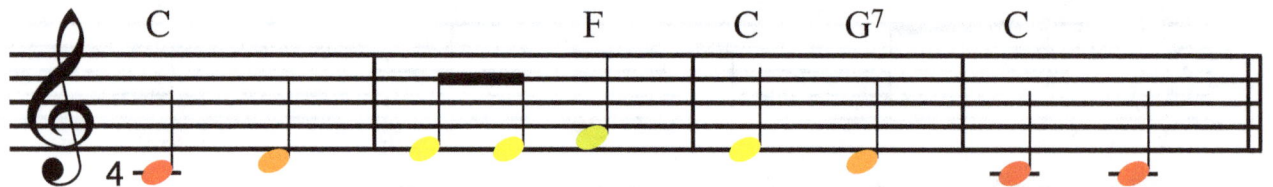

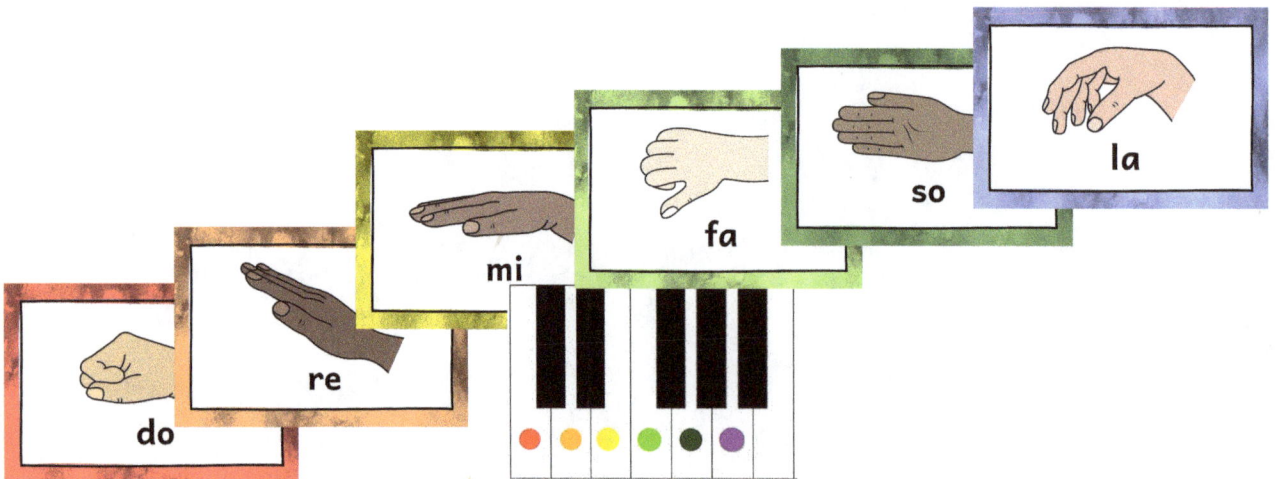

do	do	re	re	mi	fa	fa	mi	mi re	do

mi	fa	so	la	la	so	fa	mi

do	do	do	do	do	do do do do	do

do	re	mi	mi	fa	mi re	do do

I am Learning to Regulate

Music: Japan (Kaeru nota ga)

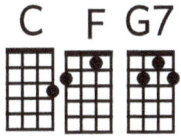

If you're in the green zone you're rea-dy to go. Yel-low zone, you might need to slow. Red zone, you need to stop and take a break. I am lear-ning to re - gu - late.

Piano Chords & Intervals

Seconds

do re mi fa so la so fa mi re do

Thirds   Fourths   Fifths

do mi so mi fa re   mi la so re   so do do so

Guitar Chords key of C

C   F   G7

Bibliography

Books

Adler, D. (1996). *The Kids' Catalog of Jewish Holidays*. Jewish Publication Society.

Bronstein, H. (1974). *A Passover Haggadah*. Central Conference of American Rabbis.

Burleigh, H.T. *Negro Spirituals arranged by H.T. Burleigh*. Art Song Central.

Campbell, P. (2014). *Music in Childhood from Preschool through the Elementary Grades*. Cengage Learning.

Carpenter, D. (2001). *African American Heritage Hymnal: 575 Hymns, Spirituals, and Gospel Songs*. GIA Publications.

Church of God in Christ Publishing Board. (1982). *Yes, Lord! Hymnal*. Church of God in Christ Publishing House.

Emmerson, J. (2014). *The Complete Illustrated Children's Bible*. Harvest House Publishers.

Hayes, R. (1948). *My Songs Panels 1, 2 & 3*. Little Brown and Company.

Giovanni, N. (2009). *On my journey now: Looking at African-American history through the spirituals*. Candlewick Press.

Glover, S. (1845) *History of the Norwich Sol-fa*. Norwich: Jarrold & Sons.

Musleah, R. (1999). *Why On This Night: A Passover Haggadah for Family Celebration*. Simon & Schuster.

Nicholls, K. (2020). *My Favourite Bible Stories For Children Around the World*. Harper Collins Publishers.

Orozco, J. (1994). *De Colores and Other Latin-American Folk Songs*. Puffin Books.

Various. (2002). *The Complete Jewish Songbook*. Transcontinental Music Publications.

White, C. (2006). *Tryin' to Get Ready: 30 African American Spirituals Arranged for SATB Voices*. GIA Publications.

Wilcox, C. (2003). *He Mele Aloha: A Hawaiian Songbook*. 'Oli'Oli Productions, L.L.C.

Zondervan. (2005). *The Beginner's Bible*. Zonderkidz.

Bibles

Aramaic Peshitta New Testament Translation. (2006). Light of the Word Ministry.

Bauscher, G. (2007) *HPBT Holy Peshitta Bible Translation*. Lulu Publishing.

Smith, J. (1876) *Smith Literal Translation*. Hartford American Publishing Co.

Websites:
www.bethsnotesplus.com

www.biblehub.com

www.mamalisa.com

www.easypronunciation.com

www.internationalphoneticassociation.org

www.ipanow.com

www.michaelkravchuk.com

www.stepbible.org

Special Thanks to Individuals

Katie African at Fivrr - Book Front & Back Covers

Daniele Leano - Português pronunciation

Priscilla Ozodo-Acevedo - voice coach and friend who has encouraged me so much in this project

Marie Polynice – Kreyòl Ayisyen (Haitian-Creole)

Christina Sanchez – Español pronunciation and sister and friend

Andriana Seay – voice coach and friend who has also encouraged me and helped me with singing

My wonderful husband, daughters, parents and sisters!

About Sarah Samuelson

Sarah Samuelson earned a Bachelor in Music Education from the University of Puget Sound, a Masters in Music Ed from Minnesota State Univ, and National Board Certification in Early Childhood Music Education. She has 15 years experience teaching music education in public schools and 6 years of teaching music education courses at the University of Puget Sound. She shared the ways that she adapted curriculum for the music classes for special education students she taught and for students with 504 plans. She has also used her skills in languages to meet needs of multilingual learners. In her private studio, Sarah has continued to learn from students with special needs, including students with Autism spectrum disorder, Trisomy 21 (Down syndrome), and students with language impairment. Combining these areas of knowledge and experience, Sarah created Learn to Sing in Harmony, a song-based method with an empathy theme to learn to read music for schools and homeschool learning. The curriculum is based on Kodaly method and incorporating folk songs from many different countries and African American spirituals from the United States and notes use the colors of the popular boomwhackers and recorders. Learn to Sing in Harmony Bible version for Christian-based learning and it follows the stories in multiple children's Bibles so that there is a song for every story. Since 2020 she has been participating in monthly Courageous Conversations (based on the Glenn Singleton book and curriculum) led by Dr. Connie Sims, reading books and watching movies and documentaries to increase her awareness and understanding of racial inequality. The books have four levels and progress in music theory with the goal being the joy of harmony! Sarah studied classical singing in her undergrad and grad programs and has performed in operas and musicals. She has been continuing her vocal growth learning new technique from vocal coaches, Onyedikachi Priscilla Ozodo-Acevedo and Andriana Seay, to sing outside of the classical genre and style especially in the areas of multiethnic & gospel worship and jazz.

More Learn to Sing & Play in Harmony Books

Learn to Sing Bible Versions

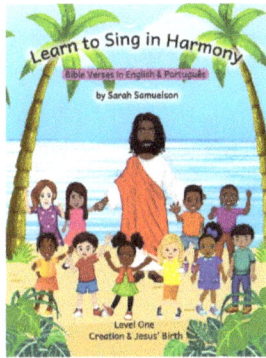

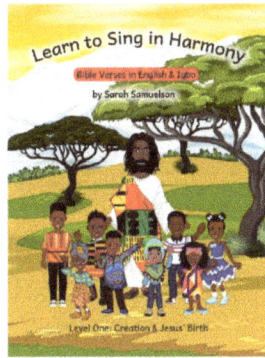

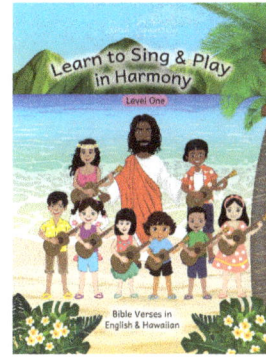

Learn to Play Recorder Books

Empathy Books for Schools

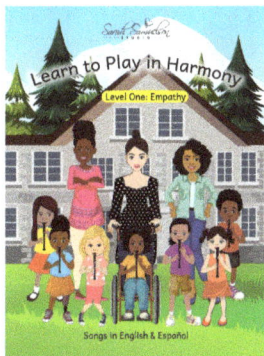

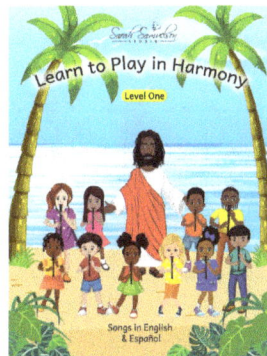

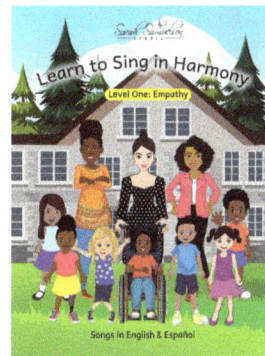

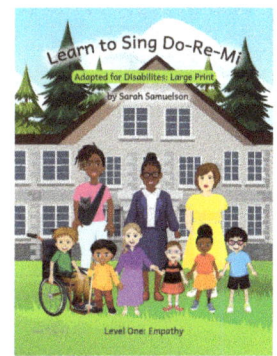

Jump-start Versions

Adapted for Disabilities

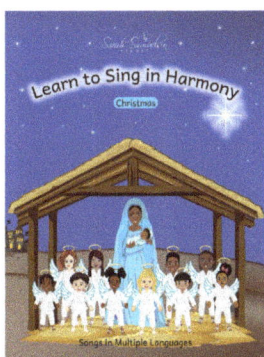

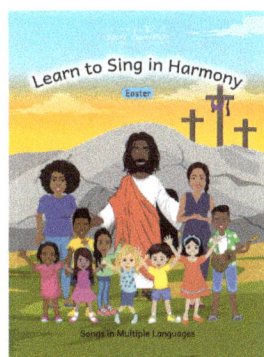

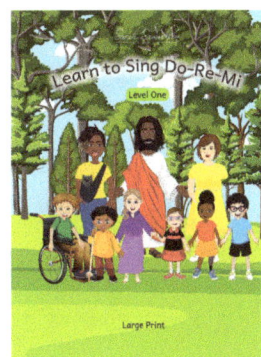

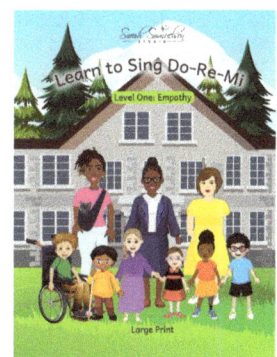

Date	Assignment	M	T	W	Th	F	S	S

Date	Assignment	M	T	W	Th	F	S	S

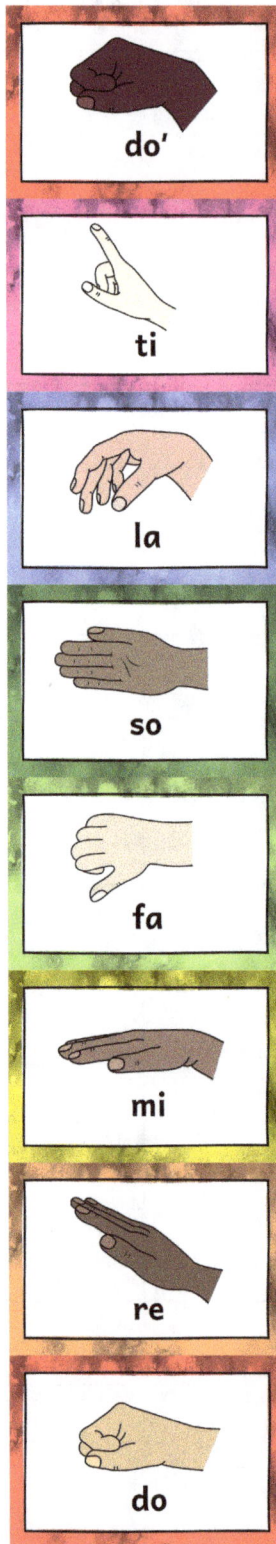

do'

ti

la

so

fa

mi

re

do